About the Author

E.J. Williot (they/she) is a queer Native American writer and Citrus Eyes is their debut poetry book. Emerald lives in a small town in Northeast Wisconsin, USA. They have many aspirations and goals for their life which includes being an author but so much more. This is her startup and it's just the beginning, she is almost completed with her Associate of Art in Humanities. They are a mental health advocate and a Human Rights and Environmental Activist. You can find more information about them on her Instagram @e.j.williot.

CITRUS EYES

E.J. WILLIOT

CITRUS EYES

Olympia Publishers
London

www.olympiapublishers.com
OLYMPIA PAPERBACK EDITION

Copyright © E.J.Williot 2024

The right of E.J.Williot to be identified as author of
this work has been asserted in accordance with sections 77 and 78 of
the Copyright, Designs and Patents Act 1988.

All Rights Reserved

No reproduction, copy or transmission of this publication
may be made without written permission.
No paragraph of this publication may be reproduced,
copied or transmitted save with the written permission of the publisher,
or in accordance with the provisions
of the Copyright Act 1956 (as amended).

Any person who commits any unauthorised act in relation to
this publication may be liable to criminal
prosecution and civil claims for damage.

A CIP catalogue record for this title is
available from the British Library.

ISBN: 978-1-83543-325-6

This is a work of fiction.
Names, characters, places and incidents originate from the writer's
imagination. Not all poems are suggested for certain readers who
have had severe mental health issues in the past or present. The
author does not endorse the themes nor romanticize them.

First Published in 2024

Olympia Publishers
Tallis House
2 Tallis Street
London
EC4Y 0AB
Printed in Great Britain

Dedication

I dedicate this book to my child and teenage self.

Synopsis

Citrus Eyes is a collection of poems that relay the hapless brain of a hopeless romantic.
The poems are individually created and have meaning behind them all. Some are satire, some are complete works of fiction, and most are simply me. I would like to think of myself as a relatable person, so take a read for yourself and see if I'm right

Hate

The world is full of hate.
But that doesn't mean you have to be full of hate.
The negativity is fuelled by the hate.
Your positivity could negate the hate.

Love

Love can negate the hate.
Love can shower people with sorrow.
Love shows the world it can be saved
Love isn't always the answer, however.

Inconsistency

Staring at a blank wall
Thinking of the times I used to cherish
Now I hate those memories
They were false securities for a person who didn't know themselves
They say they hate those times yet that's the only thing they think about
An inconsistent person with an inconsistent mind.

Child Glasses

When I was a child
everything seemed so attainable
The sky seemed closer
The world seemed peaceful
The future seemed easy
Life seemed smooth
as if nothing could hinder me
Now as I grow older everything seems
unreachable
As if the sky moved far away
As If the world grew stale
As if the future became hard
The reality of it all is the latter
Even as children the world never changed
It was the glasses we wore to keep the child-like
wonder
As children we were spared
Spared the doubt and faults of our elders
The happenings of the real world
The truth of our future
What anyone would do
Just to be able to wear those glasses again

Decorate

We moved a lot when I was a kid
My room was also my sister's
We could only afford three bedrooms
We wouldn't decorate knowing it was temporary
Then I became a teenager
My sister decided the living room was best
I finally had my own room
But even before it was my own
I filled up every spot possible
Nothing was bare
I decorated
Now we have our own house
I'll be nineteen
And my walls are once again covered
My room filled with trinkets
I have stuffies; stuffed animals
It's cozy as if this was my childhood
My room is homely
To give a façade of a permanent space

Facebook Games

My parents come home
from work to play Facebook games
Their minds are clouded

All I Want

All I want is to be someone
Someone who is loved
Who is cared for
Who is appreciated
Who is wanted

All I want is to be someone
Someone who gives
Instead of takes
Someone who governs
Instead of complies
Someone who advocates
Instead of critiques

All I want is to be someone
Not another mindless body
That passes through every day
I want to be someone who makes a difference
I want to be the difference

Blatant

I loved you for all the wrong reasons
Blatant hatred
I hated you for all the wrong reasons
Blatant love
I forgot you for the right reasons
Blissful ignorance
I remembered you for the right reasons
Blissful memories

Dream

I had a dream
You were in it
Then it changed
We were together
I shouldn't have done it
I made you do it
I'm sorry to the other girl but he's mine now
It doesn't matter
I woke up.

Invisible

I see stars in your eyes
But they don't shine for me
I see happiness in your smile
But you don't smile for me
I see you
But you don't see me

Attention Getter

You've caught my attention, without intentions.
Your smile is contagious,
Your flaws are adorable.
Your socks make my day.
You're adorable and geeky.
I wish I knew what you were thinking...
what you think about me.
I'm afraid when the lights turn off
The voices are louder then
If I don't move, they can't get me
Not the voices
The manifestations of the voices
They're going to catch me.
They're going to do something.

Unreal Head

The things in my head aren't real
My imagination feels surreal
It's like I'm grounded
Instead of being trapped in my room
I'm trapped inside the prison of my mind

I don't know what to do
I'm sinking into nothingness
The abyss of my mind
Isn't like the void of the Grand Canyon while it's dark, No
It's the empty feeling you get
At three in the morning and you're walking
And it's foggy out and you can barely,
just barely see the edge of town.
It's almost like you know that something's there.
Watching your every move
Every step has eyes lurking in the thickness.

My feelings are as if I
was transported into Silent Hill
The only thing that I see is fog and mist
I would wish to see a pyramid head
Instead, I see something far worse
Me
I'm translucent and evil
As though I'm watching myself

My good self making wrong decisions
I'm watching my evil self judge
It's like I have one goal
To figure out why I'm watching myself

The translucency is metaphorical
I'm not really watching myself from the edge of the fog
I'm looking at the root cause of me being how I am.

Not evil but empty.

Distrust Mirror

The mirror's reflection isn't you
The mirror's reflection isn't you
Cover it back up
Cover it back up
Get out of it's sight
Get out of it's sight
They're going to take you
They're going to take you

Death is Coming

The wind is roaring
Death is coming
Blackbirds are soaring
Death is coming

The wind is singing
The trees are dancing
The birds are singing
The people are dancing

The wind is silent
Death is coming
Blackbirds are resting
Death is coming

No time to stop
No one to see
Stay sheltered
You are safe here

The wind is roaring
Death is coming
Blackbirds are soaring
Death is coming

Death is coming
Death is coming

Blackbirds are droning
The wind is roaring
Blackbirds are circling
The wind is slowing

Death is here
Death is taking
Death has come
Death has taken

In Between

I want to go to the ocean
Sit in the sand all alone
As I look forward at the vast unknown
I will think to myself
I am tiny… Nothing to be seen here
As the stars engulf the night sky
I will lie down still alone
As I look upward at the vast unknown
I will know that the stars were aligned for me
I am big… Everything is to be seen
I am my own company until I look back to the
sea. At the horizon my worlds collide
The world where I am tiny
And the world where I am big
Collide and merge into the world I am in
It's a matter of I am both
I am tiny compared to some others
I am big compared to some others
And well, I am simply me
The one who is in love with the stars for they give
me the confidence to see myself

People Watching

Sitting in my 18th-floor hotel room gazing out of the window
People living on the street
Walking and moving about the bustling city
The apartment complex across my window
People living in expense
A woman contemplating her life
I'm assuming
A woman taking care of her baby
I'm assuming
A couple watching true crime TV
I'm assuming
A couple walking their dogs
I'm assuming
A woman running down the street
She's late for a date
I'm assuming
A man living alone
I'm assuming
They can see me
I'm assuming
I can see them

Unfair

It's not fair that some people can be happy when I can't.
It's not fair that some people have love when I don't.
It's not fair that some people are healthy when I'm not.
It's not fair that people are living when I'm barely getting by.
It's not fair that some people can see the world when I'm stuck where I'm at.
It's not fair that some people are successful when I'm not.
It's not fair.
It's just not fair.
When will I have happiness?
When will I have love?
When will I be healthy?
When will I live?
When will I see the world?
Tell me when!

I Miss Those Days

I miss the days when I didn't have to worry about a credit card
I miss the days when I didn't have to worry about a loan
I miss the days when I didn't have to worry if my semester was paid for
I miss the days when I didn't have to worry about the next paycheck
I miss the days when I wasn't an adult
I miss the days when I didn't need a job but wanted one
I miss the days when I could sleep all day and stay awake all night during the summer
I miss the days when I could write fanfiction all night
I miss the days when my biggest worry was if I could have the TV to watch the new episode of my show
I miss the days when I was a kid
Those are the days I miss

~~Lover~~ Stranger

I love you even though I don't know you
I'm a young woman who's waiting for your love
One day we'll find each other
That day will be absolute bliss
When that happens you'll know
When that happens I'll already know that I love you
Whoever you are
Wherever you are
I love you

Depressed Brain

Do I even want to get better?
I sit alone being quiet
Even though I'm medicated
Am I even ill?
Diagnosed professionally
Even though I don't have episodes
Could I blame others?
I shouldn't
However, if I could be open
About the thoughts in my head
My brain is a depressive episode room
Thoughts scattered around like dirty clothes on the floor
Brain fog like the smell of B.O.
Dark, Intrusive, and Scary
Yet, comforting and secure
Sitting alone I wonder
Do I even want to get better?

Inescapable Brain

I hate being stuck in my head
The want for new
But the fear of it too
The want to leave
But the fear of it too
I want to travel and see
But I'm anxious too
I want to leave.
But I don't have the courage to
I want to *leave*
But I don't have the **courage** to

Courageous Coward

It's the coward's way out
Not in all cases
People who couldn't find an escape
Found **the** escape
Others projected
Finding something to occupy their mind
The way out on the back burner
Never truly forgetting their plan
But holding off on *it*

Love Paradise

You've set me free my dear,
Yet you hold me near
I'm in love with you
With you I have no fear.

Your eyes hold my favorite hue
But that's something you knew
Love of my life
Our love is true.

So far we have no strife
Our bond is stronger than a knife
You're the one who showed me real love
You are my paradise.

Darling you've set me free with your real love
I am yours
You are mine
Our love is our own paradise.

Pity

I'm not so well.
I'm better than some.
Comparing doesn't help.
I binge,
    binge,
        binge
Then pity myself after.
I pity myself like clockwork
People say "It'll be okay"
People say "It's okay to not be okay"
Okay…
Asking for help is difficult
Everything is
I wish there was something that was easy
Something that makes things easy and okay
But,
    there's nothing.

Rebirth

In order to be reborn you have to die first.
Well, what if I told you I already died.
Seems impossible right?
I'm still here…
Well, perhaps it's my meat suit, my vessel, the bag of bones that's here.
My mind and soul, however, have been dead for years.
It's time to be reborn.
Change the meat suit that you currently see Into something… more me.
My soul died and has been reborn.
If you'd care to notice my change in demeanor.
My mind died and has also been reborn.
You would've been able to tell if you listened.
Listen to how I now choose my words more carefully and precise.
Listen to the unspoken words that I say when I don't speak at all.
Now it's time for you to really see the change.
I'll become a new person.
Change how I dress, how I hold myself.
Change my hair, perhaps I'll wear contacts.
I'll change the way that I let people bully me around.
I'll become a totally new person who is banned from my old self's memories

That's how you become reborn.
Without truly dying first.

I'm the Moon

I feel like the moon
I go in phases
I cause tidal waves
I disrupt emotions
I bring good deeds
I bring bad times
I reveal certain parts of me
I feel like the moon

SAD

The sun fades faster making my brain sputter
Becoming stagnant and slow
Going deeper into the cold
The sun fades slower
My brain's in the microwave
Warming up to new alertness
Ready to move
Ready to live

Sunflower

Unlike the sunflower I don't look at the bright side
I sulk in the shitty moments
I bitch and complain about a lot of things
I don't even preach happiness to others
It's tiring
The constant negativity I endure all on my own
My fault too for that
A sunflower will always find the sun
No matter the weather their world is the sun
In the darkness of storms they look toward the seemingly non-existent sun
As for me in my constant eternal storm, the sun is non existent
Simply non-existent
The sunflower lives peacefully knowing there is always sunshine
I live on edge never knowing if I'll find my sun
I hate sunflowers because I know I'll never be a sunflower

False Memories

I hate how it's fake.
They were supposed to be real.
Now they're memories

What If?

I think about you sometimes
The time we could have shared
It's silly honestly
You probably don't think of me
Which is okay
I can be forgettable
I wonder about the times when you asked
And I laughed it off
Thinking it was a joke
Your eyes had hurt in them
Or maybe I'm just making that part up
Either way I wonder
If I would have said yes
What we would be now
Together?
Maybe?
Or would we have cut ties, moved on
and forgot?
It's the 'what-ifs' that fill my head
Especially when I overthink every conversation
we had
I should've said 'yes'
But instead I was looking at someone else
Knowing he didn't like me
But I had more hope with him
Than you

Should've Been Us

It was supposed to be you and me
We were going to take the world by storm
Something happened that I will never understand
I wish we'd communicated better
Now you're gone

Cotton Candy Sky

Cotton candy skies
Why don't I fall for good guys?
Cotton candy skies in the night time
Cotton candy sky
When will I find the right guy?
Cotton candy skies
No more bad guys

Fictionally Real

She looked at him in more than a friend way
He did the same, both are oblivious
And so neither wanted to even say
That the two wanted each other; lascivious

Now together they knew it was true love
Although seemed to be lustful at the start
It became true and their love went above
And they know now that they own each other's heart

Above all they knew they couldn't be apart
So the end isn't near they're now married
Their love has inspired pieces of art
The art meant that their love will be forever carried

Even though others saw their love as fictional
They knew that it was real and unconditional.

Letter to the Ones I've Hurt

Dear you,
I'm reaching out to say that
I know I've hurt you in the past
I know you didn't deserve it
I knew what I was doing
We were kids
Kids are dicks sometimes
Except for me
It was malicious
Filled with intent and no remorse
I'm sorry
You don't have to accept
However, I apologize
Sincerely, me

An Apology

I am sorry
You don't have to accept it
Just know that I am sorry
I was mean to you I know I was
There's no excuse
Just an apology

Friendship

Best friends…
We were so close
This was new to me then…
And it's foreign to me now

I let you slip
I've made dumb mistakes

We didn't need each other
It was nice
Now you're with others
While I'm alone

Jesalynn

My dear friend
With all the love I give you I am at another halt
For I have to hoist another white flag
Not from the lack of love
Fear not from that
For this poem shall lay peace
For this is the one true way
Expression of love in written form
Far greater than any other.

Circus Freaks

The circus came to an end.
Time for carnies and freaks to descend.

What will happen to them?
As they wonder, fidgeting with their hem.

They'll be ridiculed and shamed.
They see it as hated fame.

Until they realized they're hated
Deep down they knew it was fated.

Nothing will change societies' minds,
About the ones who are carnies and freaks as defined.

Forever gone,
When realization dawn

That we're all circus freaks,
Just waiting for critiques.

DV

Boom! Clap! Boom!
The child hears from the other room
Ahh! Stop! Ahh!
The child whimpers with her mother's scream
Boom! Clap! Boom!
Rings through the house again
Boom! Bang! Boom!
The child doesn't hear her mother
Boom! Stomp! Boom!
The child hears her father's footsteps
Boom!
Her father slams the door open
Wooo-ooo! Wooo-ooo! Wooo-ooo!
The child faintly hears
Click! Pop! Bang!
The child hears no more.

Dreamer's Suicide

My head won't hit the pillow tonight
It'll hit the pavement
Subconsciously jumping in my dreams
As I'm falling head-first into the seas

Serotonin Dreamland

I had a dream that everything was right in the world
That you and me; we were together
I was happy
You were happy
Everyone was happy
My dream was a serotonin wonderland
Oh! How I wish it wasn't a dream

Lonesome Friend

She never had a group of friends before
She promised she would make them proud; they tore.

She was never good with her emotions
Feels, she has deemed them as useless notions.

Now they are gone, her feelings and her friends
She says, "feelings are useless,"
and "friends end."

But

The day comes to an end
I'm glad that you're here
But I need you to leave
I know,
Buts throw everything out
That was said prior
Now leave
I don't want to ask again
I need to let go
Stop the dwell
And let loose
Let me free
Please.

Moving On

Life gives
Death takes
That's how the world goes 'round
You see it with the trees
You see it with the seas
You see it with the animals
And you see it with the humans
It's a constant in an inconsistent world
Live your life as you wish
Maybe in death you can move on further

Pathetic Feelings

I took your words to heart
In which I felt I wasn't enough
In which I felt you were the one
Pushed back into reality
How foolish
How naive
How sad of me
You were never there
You will never be there

A Young Couple

Wandering the aisles of Walmart
Young couple holding hands
Their hands placed unusually
Her's behind her back
His hand connected with hers
Those two muttering sweetness
They kissed afterwards both giggling
Back to wandering

Brown Meets Blue

He was hers
She was his

He was her everything
She was his everything

He was beauty
She was chaos

She was happiness
He was sadness

She was his everything
He was her everything

She became someone else's
He sank

She hollowed him
He allowed it

She promised him, a lie
He accepted the promise as truth

He fell
Deeper, Farther, Slower,
Then faster into the abyss

Finally the sun shined on him again
Her light, amber-brown eyes
Complemented his piercing, ocean-blue eyes

Their gazes are like the crashing waves of the Hudson
and Atlantic
Her beauty in his sorrow they were meant to be

STOP

All of the stars
Each of them as far, as I feel from you
Calls and texts come in few

Do you not love me?
Do you long to be free?
Please come back
I didn't lose track,
Of the time you didn't call
I don't want us to fall

Baby please reply
I'm losing my air supply
You gave me breath
Now you're giving me death

You're still my true love
Why aren't I yours?
Is she prettier? Is she smarter? Is she better?
Am I just not good enough?

My heart is shattering
Stop my heart from pattering

Then stop.

Contradictory

Her eyes full of pain
The apples of her cheeks are tear-stained
Her petite face stolid
"What's wrong? How are you?" many ask
She gives only a shrug, saying,
"Nothing, I'm fine."

As days go by, her face becomes stone
She glares at the entire world
No one knows why
Her heart is like Antarctica
Cold.
Dry.
Empty.

She's an icy January storm
Her bitter cold aura envelopes the world
Then all at once
All at once it's suddenly warm
She's suddenly warm

He is a contradiction
A contradiction to her arctic winter
He is a warm summer

First Dance

He smiles at me and I smile back
He takes my hand and we dance
I don't like the attention but he holds me close
"Just close your eyes" he tells me
"I can feel their stares," I say back
My eyes open and I stare into his
"Whose stares, dear? It's just us."
He smiles, I give an incredulous look
We laugh.
He spins me out then pulls me close
I close my eyes
Bury my face in his neck
"I love you" I say
"I love you my dear"
I can feel the vibrations of him saying it back.

No Frets

As the world burns with pity and sorrow
I have little time to borrow
As the world burns to ashes and regrets
I have one final fret
That I will be the one filled with pity
That I will be the one filled with sorrow
For I have no more time to borrow
I'm the ash that the world has become
I'm the one without any final regrets
No need for these frets

Reminds Me of You

Storms make me think of you
The lightning reminds me of our spark
The thunder reminds me of our laughs
The rain reminds me of our shared pain
The hail reminds me of our punch buggy games
The wind reminds me of your voice
Storms make me think of you

Live or Die

To live is to die
There is no rhyme or reason to a maddening world
Unless of course there is a deeper meaning

Sightings are indifferent to some
But maybe that's what I need.

It's as though they don't want me to believe
but want me to at the same time

I need sightings to help me
When will they know that,
telling is different from seeing.

You walk until you can't any more
Constant motion

But when will you start living
And if you told me that
"To believe is to live"
Then I don't want part in your beliefs

I'd rather die than be alive.

Drowning Love

I'd rather burn in the flames of a thousand suns
than drown in oceans of your tears
The flames would engulf me while I scream in
agony when I choose to burn
Your tears would envelope me
as they pull me to the depths of your despair
and drown me without letting me get a single
sound out if I chose to drown
The flames would give me a voice
Your tears would silence me
That my love is why I decided that I shall burn
instead

Nightmare Dreamscapes

I've been dreaming
My entire life nothing but a dream
A figment of my imagination
To rid the bad
One dreamscape to another
Until one day I finally woke up
Realization occurs
Those dreams were real after all
However they weren't dreams
Rather they were nightmares
Countless nights anxiety stricken
Having me in a choke hold
I was gasping for breath
People around me were in dreams
They had beautiful dreams
I was dragged through hell
As they frolicked and breathed

Insecurities

I gaze upon myself
Tears rolling down
I hate what I see
The *thickness* of my
Face,
Arms,
Stomach,
and Legs
I force a smile to myself
I hate what I see
The snaggletooth,
Discolored– yellowed teeth
Crooked lips envelop them
The forced smile falls
I hate what I see
The features of the family
I want nothing to do with

I Wish I Was

I wish I was Pretty enough
I wish I was Native enough
I wish I was Smart enough
I wish I was Brave enough
I wish I was Loved enough
I wish I was Nice enough
I wish I was There enough
I wish I was Present enough
I wish I was Small enough
I wish I was Enough

She's a Knight

She places her pen on her paper
Tear tracks line her cheeks
Inhaling a
Long,
Deep,
Breath.
She writes...
A whole new world
For the ones who understand
For the ones who don't

Well,
They'll understand soon
She details it with doodles on the side
Giving her work a painful grin
She signs it leaving her sword and shield
As she defeated her enemy
So she can face a new one

The Giving In

I'm giving in
I'm giving in
I'm giving in to you
Your temptation of safety
I fell into the chasm of love
You're still standing at the top
You didn't fall with me
You didn't fall in love with me
You stayed grounded
I gave in
I gave in
I gave in to you

Disaster Love

I'm naive to think
I'm on the brink
Of creating my own disaster
My thoughts are racing faster
You drew me in
Nobody is going to win
I let go
You stay anchored
Dragging me back
I'm losing track
Of time
Finally we both release
Unexpected
Our love isn't decease.

Happiness

What is happiness?
I could give you a textbook definition but what's the point?
It's something that everyone experiences differently.
No matter what you say,
Someone out there will not feel happy from it.
A 'how to' guide isn't going to make everyone happy.
It may make some but not all.
See now for some seeing puppies and kittens make them happy.
For others it's a comedy or laughing with friends.
There's not a sure way to give people happiness.
Not even the kindest of gestures can make some happy.

Napalm Dream

You were holding my hand as we're in the sand

Napalm blasting around us
"It's fine" you murmur
We accepted our fate
"I...I love you," I stutter

I woke up
Monotonous alarm drones on
I frown
Realizing that you're fictitious

Four Seasons

Your warm embrace is like
the June sun with it's warm breeze;
Nice and comforting

Then Autumn; the fall.
Tension rise with the crisp air.
Once tense but it leaves.

Summer to Autumn.
Change the inevitable.
Autumn to Winter

Your embrace cold like December's wind and
blizzards
Season change again.

Your embrace lingers.
Like April's rain showers do.
People are seasons.

They change and alter.
The change alerts new people.
The one: four seasons

Love an Open Notion

Love is an open notion
An idea, an emotion
Serendipity, bliss, and unreason
Comes with your treason
Your cart on the rollercoaster kept going,
As mine slowed and halted
Why don't you love…
Us?
Me?
Yourself?
This treason brought,
Chance, joy, and unreason
It's an idea, an emotion
Love, the open notion

Apathetic Empathy

I'm apathetic
You're empathetic
Yet when I'm with you I become empathetic
Yet when you're away from me you become apathetic

Honey I don't want you to have apathy
I've known apathy my whole life
Because of you I'm now familiar with empathy
You make me feel empathy
Don't feel apathy because of me

Abused Love

I wanted to be yours
But you wanted nothing to do with me
I finally forgot about you
Then you wanted me to be yours
I wanted to be yours again
You abused me
You broke me
You're not the person I fell for
All those years ago you were
Humble
Kind
Caring
Now you're different you're
Chaotic
Aggressive
Abusive
I hate you

First Dance II

He spins me slowly
Then dips me lowly
He bends down slightly
And kissed me lightly

August 2016

Rain and teardrops intertwined.
Why did you do this?
Please rewind.
We can't take this pain
We can't take this hurt
Our prayers aren't answered.
Our prayers aren't heard.
Death reaped an unripened soul

Wish we could rewind.
Wish we could rewind

The life that was taken.
Death must be mistaken.
It wasn't your time
I want to erase time.
Why did you do this?
Death took you
Now you're his.
Maybe he wasn't mistaken

You let this happen.
You caused all the pain
You knowingly sent us all through hell.
It's your fault.

My Grave

I walk leisurely through
Glancing at just about every headstone.
The leaves crunch under each step.
The wind howls, making more leaves fall.
The crunch lessens; sinking into fresh earth.
I glance at the shiny headstone.
It reads my name.
D.O.D today.

The howl of the wind ends.
I take a step backward into a tree.
No
Can't be.
The tree isn't that close.
It was something
It was someone
The branch feels different.
The wind howls again
I take a step forward onto the once fresh earth
I turn around to be met with my friend
I turn back to the headstone
It was once shiny
Now it's dull and mossy.
I fell back into the earth

Love if for Gaia

I wanted to be in love so badly
But I know I'm not ready
Instead, I took to the trees,
the swamps, the hills, and the waters
The earth is unconditional and will love until it implodes
The earth will give until it needs to take
The earth needs to take now and I can see that
The ravens and crows bring omens of sorrow
But also act as messengers
Gaia is in need and no one cares
Gaia has an inability and that's what we need to find
It's time we give her stability

Gaia Needs Healing

Mother Nature wants love,
But we pollute her with
plastic, Landfills, greenhouse gasses, and more kill her.
When will we learn that she isn't made of elastic?
Gaia, another word for earth.
She gives us a home and life.
Pollution kills more than what we can replace.
Humankind brings uproar;strife.

Veganism and recycling are little variations of help But she needs more than that to survive
Changing the capitalistic minds may help in the long run
Less pollution, less fossil fuels will help her revive.
In the end we all need to change
Less Carbon footprints and single-uses
Will better everyone's well-being
So then we can heal her bruises.

The Rock in the Sky

I've always been drawn to him.
I've always been drawn to her
I've always been drawn to them.
Whether you associate masculine energy.
Whether you associate feminine energy.
Whether you associate fluid energy
I've always been drawn to them.
I've always been drawn to her
I've always been drawn to him.
Daylight doesn't stop the attraction.
Nighttime strengthens the attraction
If you haven't realized who I'm talking about
Perhaps I shall suggest you pay attention
Pay attention to the small things in life.
They're bigger than you think

Shakespearean Existentialist

"To be or not to be?"
It's an existential question.
To be what you're supposed to be.
Not to be what you're supposed to be.
Which do you choose?
Is it to be or is it not to be?
The real question is
'WHO are you supposed to be?'
Or
'WHO are you not to be?'
Shakespeare was built on iambic pentameter phrases
"To be or not to be"
"Love is blind"
What's an applicable Shakespeare phrase that fits identity crises or self-preservation questions?

How can one truly say Shakespeare is full of relatable quotations when he is full of 17th-century notations?

I am to be me.
And I am not to be Shakespeare.
That's the answer.

End of an Era

It's sad
Watching everything that shaped you
Into the person you are today
End or slowly end
The eras in which shaped you ends

Weird Kid

Mommy always said to make friends with the weird one
But what if I'm the weird one, Mommy?
You said to make friends with the lonely kid at the lunch table
Who was eating and reading; earbuds in
But Mommy I am that kid
I'm the kid who sat alone at the lunch table
With a book in my hands and music in my ears
Well, I wasn't alone completely
I had pets, people who'd give me food
People who were so compliant that I was a Queen
People not pets
I was the pet
I was the weird kid that their mommies told to befriend

Chaos Looks for Peace

Well, she is chaos
Looking for peace within her.
Or maybe in him.

__Night and Day__

Her smile was like the sun.
It was bright and full of life.
His eyes shined bright as the night stars.
They were night and day in that sense.

She is Ash

Their fire roared on for millions of years
He left her in ashes when he left this world

Always People Watching

I look at the world every day
How it has multiple personalities on display
Everyone has their own life with an array
Not everyone is what they lay
Some are good, some are not
Don't be displeased,
We're all taught that some have it easy,
some have fought
We're all people-watching;
in our own thoughts